By Way Of Your Heart

PALMETTO
PUBLISHING
Charleston, SC
www.PalmettoPublishing.com

By Way Of Your Heart
Copyright © 2024 by Priscilla Sands

All rights reserved

No portion of this book may be reproduced, stored in a retrieval system, or transmitted in any form by any means–electronic, mechanical, photocopy, recording, or other–except for brief quotations in printed reviews, without prior permission of the author.

Paperback ISBN: 979-8-8229-2686-8
eBook ISBN: 979-8-8229-2687-5

By Way Of Your Heart

A collection of poems by
Priscilla Sands

For my son Donnie Stamps
August 17, 1969 to April 29, 2022

Who anchored me to this world and fueled my
determination when I was not sure
I could battle another storm.
You inspired this book with your faith in me.
My love for you pushed me through to the end.
I couldn't do it for myself, but I would do
anything for you.
And though time will travel on without you.
You will not be forgotten.
These pages will carry your memory through time.
So I did it.
This is for YOU

Table of Contents

AUTHORS NOTE 1
BY WAY OF YOUR HEART 2

MIXED EMOTIONS 5
  A STRANGER LED 6
  MAGIC 7
  THINK OF ME 8
  SWEET DREAMS 10
  NOBODY'S LAUGHING 11
  IF YOU LEAVE ME ALONE 13
  THE CHAMBER DOOR 14
  I DON'T UNDERSTAND 15
  I WONDER 17
  WHEN 18
  MY FRIEND 19
  SPLATTERED PICTURE 21
  NEW YEARS DAY 1982 22
  MIXED EMOTIONS 24
  AT YOUR KITCHEN TABLE 26
  REFLECTIONS 28
  MAN BEHIND THE WHEEL 30
  IT'S OVER 31
  KNOWING 32
  INTROSPECTION 33
  COUNTRY ROADS 34
  YOU'LL NEVER KNOW 36
  BLUE EYES 37
  BREAK OF DAY 38
  GAMES 39
  TO THE HUMAN RACE 40
  THE END 41

FOREVER SOFTLY IN MY HEART 43
THE STRANGER AND THE LADY 44
HOLD ME 45
LOVE IS NEVER IN VAIN 46
A WALK THROUGH PRISMS 47
TO ROBERT GUY 48
FOREVER SOFTLY IN MY HEART 50

IN REMEMBRANCE 53
PRAYER FOR MY SON 56
THERE ARE NO WORDS 58
HE BRINGS ME SUNFLOWERS 60
THERE'S NO ONE TO CALL ME
    MOM ANYMORE 62
THE DAY I LOST FLYNN 64
TO FLYNN 65
THE DOOR WAS ALWAYS OPEN 67

FROM SOLDIER TO PASTOR 68

IN MY FANTASIES 73
IF THE WORLD WERE ONLY YOU AND I 74
YOU AND ME AND SWEET THINGS 75
CRYSTAL SHIP 76
BUILDING CASTLES 78
COME PLAY WITH ME 80
I DANCED FOR YOU 81
MY JOURNEY'S END 82

ACKNOWLEDGEMENTS 84

AUTHORS NOTE

This book is only bits and pieces of a story that took a lifetime to write.

Love is mentioned too often in these poems but it is what I have learned from that which matters.

Most of the loves in our lives are just passing through. Their names and faces will be buried in time and long forgotten memories.

But there will be a few who pass through slowly and they will carve out a space in our heart, where the love that was shared can dwell for a lifetime.

BY WAY OF YOUR HEART

Your spirit is yours alone
It cannot be bound by others desires
Remember always … there will be a light
At the end of a path taken
When you travel by way of your heart

MIXED EMOTIONS

A STRANGER LED

I traveled on spirits of gypsies wings
Through winds of change time often brings
To find that every chamber door
Behind, was closed forever more

So I traveled on, and the blackbird sings
As the bell in the distant tower rings

Until one dreary autumn eve
A stranger led not to deceive
Down yet another corridor
Fraught with mysteries as before

And the blackbird in the window sings
What a peace and comfort to me it brings

But then I turned to find the stranger gone
And could hear no more the blackbird's song
A bolted castle door behind
Brought fear, that left it hard to find

A way back to the gypsies wings
And the blackbird … he no longer sings

MAGIC

We are a prism you and I of ever changing hues
With colors of intensity we have never known
And emotions there may be no aura for

Should we pass this prism together
Let us travel slowly
Not to miss a single subtle changing

For after our passing and beyond
When we look to find our colors fade to black
Do not fear what lies ahead

It is magic that begins and ends in darkness

THINK OF ME

When darkness gives way to dawn
And you leave my arms again
Though your need for me is gone
Think of me now and then

When it seems the sky has swallowed your sun
And the moon has come to haunt you
If you find there's nowhere else to run
Think of me, I'll see you through

SWEET DREAMS

Though I am here alone tonight
My thoughts are there with you
Wanting for you the sweetest dreams
Of star filled skies and moonbeams

And hoping perhaps that somewhere
Deep in your softest dreams
That I will pass through the shadows
Before your dreams are through

Stay with me for just a while
I will give you what I can
Until the winds that brought you here
Take you back again

Then will I remember
How I felt like a babe in your arms
And gathered from you the strength you gave
When it seemed that mine had gone

So when my tears have dried
And another is by my side
I'll remember the kindness you gave
When you could have turned away

Still wanting for you the sweetest dreams
Of star filled skies and moonbeams

NOBODY'S LAUGHING

You're gone now
I doubt you'll ever return
It's kind of funny
But nobody's laughing
He left a few days after you
I know you tried to say goodbye
I'm sorry I wasn't there
I guess he said goodbye for both of you
It's funny …
But nobody's laughing

IF YOU LEAVE ME ALONE

If you leave me alone
You'll see my eyes in every star that shines
Find reflections of my face in the moon
In every breeze that passes your way
Will be my arms reaching for you

If you leave me alone

THE CHAMBER DOOR

The magic light that once did loom
Has darkened now to dread and gloom
Each time these castle walls surround me
For despair hath overtaken thee

You heard the cries from chamber doors
As you traveled down the corridors
For the Raven crossed your path indeed
Though since has taken warnings heed

From queens who sit on thrones secluded
Throwing stones from heights eluded
Toward the bewildered bird of yore
Who lay below in blood and gore

Oblivious to spoken ill intent
Unaware of what her presence meant
Until a chamber door revealed
A secret which was once concealed

Yet to this day the Raven wanders
Softly past the door and ponders
For the Raven entered not… in lore
Through the King's chamber door

Not now said the Raven, nor heretofore

I DON'T UNDERSTAND

Your eyes were full of laughter then
They would smile at me
I loved you, didn't I?

Day before yesterday I saw you alone
You looked so lost
I'd never seen you like that before
I felt lost too

Today I saw you with her
The laughter I knew in your eyes was gone
The laughter in mine was returning

It's tomorrow now, I see you
Your eyes are not laughing
And neither are mine
Can you tell me why

I don't understand …
Or do I?

I WONDER

Can a stream flow into a river
A river that has been blown by many winds
And has covered many miles
Can a stream survive those miles yet to be traveled
Could there be a blending of the tides

Could you ever love me
And would you understand
Or will the winds that have blown me far
And brought me back again
Carry you away from me

Because it almost scares me to think
That I might need you
I know that nothing is certain
I only know for sure what I think
And I think I could love you

Do you ever wonder?

WHEN

I can't be sure when the feeling
Didn't feel the same
Or when I couldn't hear you
Calling my name

It must have been time after time
When … I couldn't stay held
Or day after day when …
I can't be sure …
Anymore

MY FRIEND

The emptiest words
I've ever heard
Were when you spoke
Of being my friend

You needed me
And I was there
You used me
Without reservation

When it was your turn
You heard my need
But would not answer
And did not care

You'll need me again
And I may listen
But will not answer
And will not care

My friend

I have never been so alone

                With someone

                                As I am with you

SPLATTERED PICTURE

I hated you
For not loving me
And for lying without reason

I hated you
For painting a picture of yourself
That was not clear

I hated finding
That your picture had been splattered
And cannot be replaced

I hated myself
For believing in you
And knowing better

Now, what is worse
I don't hate either of us
I just don't care

I hate that!

NEW YEARS DAY 1982

I know there's been a time
Though when I cannot say
That I have felt so alone
As I have this day

I seem to have missed the dawn
Or was it just not bright
I cannot understand
For I was not alone last night

He is a very young man
While I am very old
Maybe not in years
But experience has been cold

I know so well his pain
Yet cannot even cry
I see myself in him
Someday his tears will dry

I held him in his time of need
And listened to his lies
Awaken to his face
To only hear goodbyes

He tells me how he needs me
I listen now and then
But his need for me will die
So these words I'll say again

I know there's been a time
Though when I cannot say
That I have felt so alone
As I have this day

MIXED EMOTIONS

If sometimes I come down on you
Like the surf upon the shore
It's only because I loved you
And can't anymore

So if some days I seem angry and cold
As the winter winds are now
It might be because I can't let go
But have to somehow

And if at times I seem misplaced
As the darkness is at dawn
It's only because I thought you were there
But turned to find you gone

So now on days when I find myself alone
A single rose in the morning dew
Perhaps it's because you left me here
When you told me we were through

But if in time my heart begins to warm
Though our lives didn't go as planned
It's just because I loved you
And I'm trying to understand

AT YOUR KITCHEN TABLE

As I sit here at your kitchen table
With coffee in my hand, and watch you drive away
Knowing only a few hours separate us now
I can feel the presence of your not being here
Even now it seems I can't get enough of you to fill me in

If your arms could reach to touch the end of time
You would find me waiting there
Then you and I could have our own parade
For there can be no rain in the shelter of my fantasies
I could show you things you've never dreamed of

As we lay in meadows by the stream
I could tell you stories of waterwheels and windmills
Of mermaids riding on dolphins by the sea
Of little children and daffodils
Kittens chasing butterflies, and love that sets you free

I'm back now here at your kitchen table, with coffee in my hand
Still feeling the presence of your not being here
And still loving you just as much at your kitchen table
As I did in my dreams

REFLECTIONS

Oh the splendor of the sun in your eyes is mine
As it peeks through my window at you
Your hair a mirror as rings of gold
To reflect upon my face
I want you

When we lay embraced in a moonlit haven of silence
Your arms enfold and hide me
That I might gather strength from you
As the raging sea from the wind
I need you

If a summer rain should softly fall on me
As I gaze into waters where dreams of you and I began
I shall find in every drop
Reflections of what might have been
I love you

Though streams that use to run so free, now are standing still
As I'm looking through waters that are not clear
I can still see reflections of you and me
Reflections of what use to be
I miss you

MAN BEHIND THE WHEEL

I almost wish that I could cry
When I see the clouds just rolling by
As we drive this lonely highway
Without a single word to say

To the man behind the wheel
Despite knowing how I feel
About this man with whom I stay
Knowing the price I have to pay

IT'S OVER

As I sit in this lonely truck stop waiting
The hours keep ticking by
Knowing it's over, yet still debating
And continuing to wonder why

KNOWING

You made me love you ... knowing
And do you feel a bigger man
For causing me this pain
I tried to bid you leave

Then you led me to believe ... knowing
Now turn and watch me walk
This time I'm really going ... knowing
All along I would

INTROSPECTION

I'm going in now, and I won't be coming out
Don't try to reach me, I'm not there anymore
I fear you could not comprehend what remains
I had to go, for it's the only place
That you can never be
Where there is no light, there can be no reflections
Don't try to find me, I'm not there anymore
And I won't be coming back

COUNTRY ROADS

I have to let go now
When your touch is still warm
Your kiss is still soft
While memories are still sweet

If I should stay
Until flames fall to cinders
And memories turn to dust
It would not have been worthwhile

So when you drive these country roads
Where the fields are yellow and the deer run free
Remember a lady who couldn't love you
And chose to walk away

YOU'LL NEVER KNOW

I never voice my thoughts my fears
Because you've made it perfectly clear
If I did have something to say my dear
That you really wouldn't care to hear

BLUE EYES

When I have to face the day
Your blue eyes turn and walk away
Know that if you ever yearn
To see my funny face again
And if you miss me now and then
I'll be close enough to find
In your memories just behind
Those blue eyes

BREAK OF DAY

Why does break of day come between us
With broken words, and silent doubts?
With light that shows us truths
We've lost in darkened crowded rooms

Should we heed the warning of dawn
Or be content with words spoken
And passion succumbed to when filled with wine
Or sheltered by black of night

For time is a clock
That is not eternal
Alas, the darkness and the light
Will never be as one

GAMES

I'm trying to play the games you play
But I never did play well ...
And trying to play them your way
Is putting me through hell

TO THE HUMAN RACE

If I should never again
Look you in the eye
Speak when you pass by or smile

It's because I have experienced you
You with evil intent and vicious lies
That smiling faces cannot disguise

It is not hate that brings me here
But bitter disappointment
For all that is within you

Bitter disappointment
In you

THE END

It was the beginning …

And the end …

And it woke me in the night
To find you …

Sleeping soundly

FOREVER SOFTLY IN MY HEART

THE STRANGER
AND THE LADY

The Stranger was rugged and torn, his hair a raging flame of red
That told of passion of spirit, a fire that would burn eternal

The blaze swept softly by the lady gathering a part of her
To carry with him for a time

So though the stranger told no lies
And the lady would not love him

Every now and then she cries

Still, the lady cries

HOLD ME

Hold me …
If only for a moment
My Love

For words that can't be said
Thoughts we're not allowed
And quiet times we'll never share

Hold me my love
If only for a Moment

LOVE IS NEVER IN VAIN

I love you
Maybe only the way I love the sun
When it lights my way to you
Though I could find you
Even on the blackest night

And maybe only the way I love birds
When they sing
Flowers when they bloom in spring
And it seems they're just for me

But I love you
Enough to see you when I can
To miss you when I can't
And enough to accept what has to be
When it's time for me to set you free

So yes through all the joys we've shared
And even through my tears
It will not have been in vain
That I have loved you

For it cannot be displaced or taken from me
And is so much more than some people
Have ever known

A WALK THROUGH PRISMS

Life is a walk through prisms
Of many changing colors
We have taken a step together
Though our walk will be a brief one
There will be a changing of the hue

And time won't be still nearly long enough
For making memories to carry with us
After our prism passing
And beyond the changing of the hue

But I will … remember you

TO ROBERT GUY

I told you once that when you held me in your arms
It felt like coming home again
There were times when I left, I would have chosen to stay
But you chose not to ask

So we broke apart slowly, over time that took its toll
After weaving in and out of one another's lives
Over half a lifetime of years we spent
Until I finally found a home in another's arms

I've tried, but cannot reach you anymore
Did you finally decide to set me free
Or was it just too hard to comprehend
That maybe this really was the end

I believe we saw the crossroad coming
So I continued to travel on
But you turned to take the bend in the road
We had traveled too far to find our way home

But there has been too much time spent
And too many memories made
To lose what love we shared
We will hang on to a part of each other

A part that cannot be replaced or taken from us
We'll find reflections of memories made
In old photos, found in boxes forgotten
From a space in time that belongs to you and I

FOREVER SOFTLY IN MY HEART

If I have but one more moment in time
To steal for you and I
Or should I have many
I will forever keep you softly in my heart
And sweetly passing through my dreams
For moments that were never found
Silent thoughts we cannot share
And love forever softly
In my heart

IN REMEMBRANCE

Sometimes when I cry
I cry for all the loves I've ever known

But always when I cry …
I cry for you

For Donnie Hawkins my first love
August 17, 1950 to October 30, 1967

PRAYER FOR MY SON

I pray the rivers however strong
Carry you toward your goals
That the winds be strong behind you
To urge you on
And the sun touch you
Ever so softly
To warm your heart when it's cold

I pray should you ever find yourself in the dark
Alone and afraid
For the skies to fill with diamonds of which every facet
Will light your way with beauty and hope
And may the nightingale sing sweetly
Until the dawn of a new day

I pray these things for you my son

For you are the river that carries me
Every poem I write, I write for you
You're the single flower that bloomed
Among the weeds in my tormented garden

What a precious flower you are
To your mother
I love you

THERE ARE NO WORDS

There are no words that come to mind
For an emotion that changes but never ends
Nor a phrase in language that I can find
For a heart that never mends

There are familiar words often thrown around
For the aftermath of loss and grief
Yet not a single word is so profound
Life now a pretense, in my belief

You will wear two faces from this day on
The truth will dwell in the shadows behind
Where memories gather from years bygone
But your eyes will forever be a reflection defined

By pieces of a heart that even time will never mend
In a world that will never be the same again
Because there are no words nor way to comprehend
What it is you have lost and the emptiness within

When you have lost your child

HE BRINGS ME SUNFLOWERS

Before he passed, I never asked
The reality I could never grasp
What sign would he bring, how would I know
So when he came … he put on quite a show

Now I wait for my summer surprise that towers
Through stormy winds and summer showers
In the filtered sun of my backyard sky
For him to let me know…that he's been by

THERE'S NO ONE TO CALL ME MOM ANYMORE

I was barely sixteen when I became a Mom
It is all I have ever known
The only thing that mattered enough
To keep me bound to this cruel world

There is no one now to call from the other room
Mom … can you … Mom will you …
What do you think Mom …
Mom, I need you

I will never be Mom again
He may have been a man when he left this world
But he will always be my child,
My baby

Now there is no one to call me Mom anymore

THE DAY I LOST FLYNN

Every time you have to let go of some one
There are pieces of your heart ripped from your chest
All I know is that day I couldn't bear the pain
And all I could do was
SCREAM

TO FLYNN

As I walk down the path now silent, where we use to run and play
In the shadow of dusk, as the trees form a haunting silhouette against the sky
I hear a voice that seems to echo from a distance far away
I miss you

I speak ever so softly into the warm night wind
You were my kisses in the morning and my comfort at night
You were my companion, my joy, and my best friend

We traveled you and I over many roads and highways
Over winding mountain passes, through valleys and country fields
We strolled beside a roaring river in a cool September haze

But it is the evenings as I held you in my arms and gently kissed your head

That forged the memories forever etched in my heart and soul
The quiet moments together as I whispered
I love you

For my dog Flynn, who is forever loved beyond measure
March 17, 2006 to July 22, 2016

THE DOOR WAS ALWAYS OPEN

If I could speak
I would tell you now
Of tales from menacing streets as I roamed
Mysteries cloaked in still shades of darkness

Of lazy playful days in the sun
Butterflies in the breeze
Raindrops from above
Honeysuckle in the morning and love

And though I returned to you often
My heart and body broken
By misadventures taken
Or lessons not so easily earned

The door was always open

Arms were there to help me
When my willful ways threw fate to chance
And my spirit filled with folly
Took to wondering of mysteries untold

So if I could speak I would say to you
Neither man nor beast could ask more
Than to live and die in the arms of souls
Who love enough to set them free

And the door was always open for me

(Inspired by a friend's loss of his beloved cat Boo Boo)

FROM SOLDIER TO PASTOR

My brother passed tragically just before this book was to be published. The pain is still too fresh and the sorrow to deep to write poetic. I can only try to honor him with descriptive words and photos that will never be able to tell the full story of the amazing life he led.

He left behind a wife, a son, two grandsons, his sister, many dear friends, his horse and two dogs.

He was a man who loved his family who served his God and his country.

It was a life lived fully from beginning to end. He served in the Army right out of high school for over 20 years and retired a Warrant Officer 3. He then contracted with the army for another 20 years, as well as doing some contract work for NASA.

He was a true cowboy at heart and team roped in many rodeos throughout this country. He also participated in rodeos as a team roper while stationed in Germany. I recall a story told at the family kitchen table often where he saw a man at a rodeo strike his horse. He covered his horses eyes with his hands to shield him from the injustice. He loved his horses dearly. He had one remaining horse at the time of his death named Amigo.

He had a bucket list which included riding his Harley to Alaska and back. None of his buddies were able to be gone long enough to make the trip, so he went alone. He felt that time was running out as he got older. So at 60 years old he took off on the road to Alaska alone and returned after 34 days with so many fascinating stories to tell.

After moving to Athens Alabama he found a church where he felt he belonged. In 2012 he became the pastor of the Cowboy Church of Limestone County. He loved his church and was dedicated to his congregation. He remained the pastor of the Cowboy Church of Limestone County until the day he passed.

He was killed tragically in a hit and run while on his daily bicycle ride. So many days I wish I could go back to tell him how proud I was of the man he had become. But we always think we have more time, until we don't. And though it is hard for those of us left behind to understand. I have no doubt that he is in God's hands. I hope knowing that will give some peace to those of us left to carry on.

Charles Steven Olney
November 9, 1954 to October 18, 1923

IN MY FANTASIES

IF THE WORLD WERE ONLY YOU AND I

If time was not
And the world were only you and I
Would we love as children do
And could we dream our dreams at play
In fields of windswept clover hay

And would the mermaids lost at sea
Return to shore for you and me
And the stars that fall in the dark of night
Could they grant our every wish in flight

And would the sun shine still
On every blooming daffodil
Through warm rains as they gently fall
Can you imagine the wonder of it all

Oh, if the world were only you and I
Would we love as children do
And could we dream our dreams at play
In fields of windswept clover hay

If, my love

YOU AND ME AND SWEET THINGS

As long as there are moonbeams
And little wide eyed children's dreams
London Bridges, Kings and Queens
There will be you and me and sweet things

CRYSTAL SHIP

In your eyes are reflections of dreams
Darkened by fear, and left to die
Take my hand my love, for I was born to dream
We will sail together for the first time
Aboard my crystal ship to places unknown
Across oceans where waves are spun
Like silken threads of silver and gold
To reach a shore where dolphins play
By a castle on the bay
And as they sing to summon the moon
We will dance through the night
By the sea in the silvery light
Cast upon the shadow of my crystal ship

BUILDING CASTLES

Yes, I love you …
But I'll never tell

So if you want me
And don't find me there

I'll be alone
In the sand, by the sea
Building castles for you and me

Because, I love you …
But I'll never tell

COME PLAY WITH ME

Come play with me, I'm your toy
And I love you little boy

But if you drop me in the sand
And someone finds me where I land

Don't cry little boy,
For you were careless with your toy

I DANCED FOR YOU

I know I said I never lied
But I guess I lied a little
When I said I didn't love you
And danced to the tune of the fiddle

I danced and I danced
And the fiddle played out of tune
As I danced for you
With the man in the moon

I danced in the sand and by the sea
Amidst the giant palms nearby
And oh what folly bring
When I danced with you in the sky

The night was young the moon so full
As we danced there was such joy
I could see in the eyes of a man
The heart of a little boy

I know I said I never lied
Well I guess I lied a little
But in you I finally did confide
As we danced to the tune of the fiddle

MY JOURNEY'S END

You knew that I would go
As time began to fade
I was to set sail again
Long before you could board my ship

Please forgive me when I've gone
For I have taken from you
That which you could not give
To see my journey through

I have taken your eyes
To see for the first time
The power and the beauty
Of the distant tides at dawn

Your laughter to ring as music
Through the winds of time
And your spirit my love
To dwell with mysteries of the sea

So after my battle with raging storms
And demons of the deep
After many years have come and gone
When my journeys end is near

If you chance upon your heart once more
To find it's been misplaced
I took it to power the wind in my sails
To carry me to my journeys end

ACKNOWLEDGEMENTS

WITH LOVE AND AFFECTION

To my husband Ed who's arms I finally found a home in. Who accepted without judgement where I had been, allowed me to be myself, and remains beside me for all my journeys to come. You are the light at the end of my path.

To my son Donnie Stamps who is still my greatest inspiration in life.
Thanks for the sunflower.

And to my brother Steve Olney for being there to hold me up when I fell apart on the hardest day of my life.
And my sister-n-law Michele for always being there to help, with a kind word and sage advice.

A VERY SPECIAL THANKS TO

Nancy Mitchell for being there when I called.

Stephanie my Project Manager for her patience and understanding while I dealt with tragedies and mishaps throughout the publishing of this book. Also to Aaron and everyone at Palmetto Publishing who helped make this book possible.

Photography for the book cover, the author's photo and the photo on page 45 by Christian Sangree.
Additional photos furnished by the author.

www.ingramcontent.com/pod-product-compliance
Lightning Source LLC
LaVergne TN
LVHW041712060526
838201LV00043B/701